Launching a Career in Software Development: Make Your Resume Pop, Your Interviews Rock and Your Career Soar

James Webb

James Webb

Preface

About the Author
For the last 10 years, I've worked as a software developer and development manager across a range of top tech companies in the Seattle area with the bulk of my time at Amazon. I've been extensively involved in interviewing (over 500 tech interviews in the last 5 years), in mentoring (working with more than a dozen interns, mentoring and coaching developers, leading small and large teams), and in delivering cool technology and has grown businesses and delighted customers.

Why This Book
Software development has been a far more rewarding career than I had ever imagined in school. The rewards have been financial as well as in job satisfaction, and both of those have only grown over time. For as fantastic as software development is, based on the number of students who seek the degree I still think it is a too well-kept secret. I wanted to help students (or industry veterans looking for someone else's perspective) understand not just why software development is great but also what the path to finding a job and succeeding looks like. As I discuss preparing, interviewing, and career planning, my advice is based on my experiences in large, fast-paced companies. If you're looking to join a startup or build your own business, some of these lessons will apply but you'll need to seek out more specific advice. Even for those of you looking for big tech, this book isn't meant to be the final word on interviews, resumes, or life satisfaction, but I do hope that my exposure and experiences can serve as a guide to help you chart your way through your career in software development.

Why You Want a Career in Software Development

When you choose a career, you're probably looking for at least one of three things:

1. Money - You want a career that pays well both relative to the market and relative to the amount of training and experience you have.
2. Job satisfaction and achievement - You want to be able to have ownership, creativity, and control over your work.
3. Demand - You want to be able to find a steady job and know that you continue to gain skills that will stay relevant.

While some jobs do well on one or two of these dimensions, very few careers score as high on all of these dimensions as software development does. According to a *US News* jobs ranking (which took into account these factors and others), software development came out as the #1 Best Job of 2014. In addition to being great at meeting many of these criteria, software development is not as training-intensive as other lucrative and satisfying careers (e.g., medicine and dentistry). Often, a 4 year degree is all that you need to make it far in a top tech company. This fantastic combination of high job compensation, personal achievement, stability, and a low barrier to entry should make software development a much bigger target for students and professionals looking to make a career switch, but demand for qualified employees still outstrips supply.

Let's take a closer look at some of the many things software development has going for it.

Great Compensation

While the median income for all individuals 25+ in 2005 in the U.S. was $32,140, the median income for full-time employed bachelor's degree holders was $56,078 (U.S. Census Bureau). For computer science degree holders, the starting salary median was $61,407 in July 2009, and the median pay was $65,668 (U.S. Bureau of Labor Statistics). While computer science encompasses a wide range of jobs, the Labor Department reported that the median software developer salary was even higher at $90,060, far above the US median income.

While the average developer is making a pretty great salary even early in their career, salaries at the top tech companies are far above average. Graduates coming straight out of school with an undergraduate degree in CS at companies like Google and Amazon are earning more than $100,000 in salary and bonuses in just their first year. That can rise to $150,000 or more if you perform well and have a few years of experience. Depending on your company and how the stock is doing, your total compensation could be even higher when the market is hot.

In addition to financial compensation, all of the large tech companies are going to offer health and dental insurance, 401k matches, decent vacation and personal time, and other perks.

Job Satisfaction

Satisfaction in software development comes from a number of factors. First is the creativity and freedom to do build new things and solve problems. Creating a new application or solving a tricky problem is a rush and being able to do it in software within a matter of days or weeks makes for a much quicker turnaround than many jobs where achievement is realized only by building things in the physical world.

Software developers usually have a high level of autonomy, particularly as they progress in their careers. They may work with project managers who define what to build and managers who are there to guide their career, but many of the decisions on how they build things are left to them. That freedom keeps the job from becoming monotonous and gives a sense of empowerment to individuals in this field.

Stability

In 2012, the unemployment rate for software developers was just 2.8% and has only gone down since then. Software developers are in high demand, which is reflected in intense visa debates and high compensation. When I was a developer and had a profile on LinkedIn, I would receive multiple contacts a week from recruiters without even trying to get noticed. If you work for a top tech company, your stability increases even further. Neither Amazon nor Google has had significant layoffs since the early 2000s, and even though Microsoft has had some layoffs, someone with a top tech company on their resume is going to have no trouble getting interviews anywhere in the industry. Even people I terminated or saw terminated from the places I worked were able to turn around and find work at decent companies within weeks.

Varieties and Branching Out

While many software developers are happy to continue doing pure software development, there are a number of related career paths in the industry that you can transition to pretty easily. For those who are more business minded, working as a Technical Project Manager is a natural way to apply your tech knowledge more directly to the requirements and specifications of business problems. If you are interested in working with large amounts of data, Research Scientists and Machine Learning Scientists require a strong technical and software development background but solve quite different problems. If you enjoy mentoring and leading people, Software Development Manager is another role that puts your technical background to use as you solve not just technical problems but project and people challenges as well. Your interests may change over time but a solid foundation and experience with software development sets you up for a number of interesting alternative paths should you want something new.

More Fun than it Should Be

I was never a student who loved pure computer science. I worried that a career in development would be as boring as the theory, proofs, and math that were a large part of my CS education. While that knowledge has been important, I was very surprised at how lucky I was in the choice of a career and how much I enjoyed the tech industry. We work with smart people on significant problems and get paid a lot to do it. With as many benefits as this job has going for it, it almost seems more fun than it should be!

Getting Started: Skills You Need

In software development, you'll find people of every kind of background and every kind of personality, but there are some traits that most have in common that make them successful in a software development career. While the programming languages and development tools you use will change over time, there are a number of skills you will need regardless of the particular technology in use at any given time.

Enjoy Problem Solving - If you just like following pre-defined paths, software development probably isn't going to be for you. Software development involves solving problems on a large scale (architecture and design), on a very minute scale (line by line debugging), and every size in between. Developers who succeed are the kind that get a thrill out of this.

Comfortable with Chaos - Software development can be messy, with shortcuts taken, changing environments, and unclear requirements. Unless you are working at NASA, you need to be comfortable dealing with some ambiguity and living with some chaos.

Clear Communicators - You must at least have clear written communication skills, and you will be far more successful if you have clear verbal communication skills as well. You will have to communicate with project managers, team members, managers and sometimes even directly with customers. Clear communication isn't about being accent free, it is expressing your ideas in a way that is structured, precise, and concise.

Self Driven - One of the things that appeals to many developers is the large amount of freedom they have to control their time and effort. Developers often have freedom about what order to do things in, what time of day they work, or even if they work in the office or at home for a day. Successful developers will be able to organize their tasks without a manager or project manager looking over their shoulder and will execute on them without prompting. This is one of the hardest traits to instill in developers if they don't have it already, so there is usually very little patience at competitive companies for developers devoid of passion.

Be Right A Lot - Unlike, say, a steak that isn't quite seasoned perfectly, errors in estimation and implementation of software are often crystal clear. You need to habitually learn from your mistakes and make fewer of them to be successful. Being sloppy with code or communication will prevent your growth and make you a liability to a team.

End of School Does Not Equal End of Learning - If you aren't learning, you aren't going to keep up with teams and technology--and it will stand out. One of the interview questions that I frequently asked candidates was to tell me about something they were learning outside of their normal set of projects. Whether this was during work hours or on their own, if they didn't have an answer they usually didn't fare well on the rest of my interview or with others. You don't have to dedicate 100% of your life to things related to your career, but you do need to continue to evolve as the industry does.

High School Preparation

For many of you this time has passed, but I want to offer some advice that may help students who are considering software development but are not in college yet.

Far more than any specific subjects to study, while you are young you should find ways to let yourself enjoy learning. Find pleasure in picking up new skills and in producing quality work. This extends beyond just academics and applies to sports, clubs, music, and other pursuits. You are going to spend a career in thinking and building so start appreciating the pleasure that comes from doing those things well.

In your software development education, there are some areas of preparation that begin in high school. The most important skill you can develop is the ability to concretely solve problems. Social sciences are valuable to life and to your career, but being able to solve problems in an exact and repeatable way is a skill that you simply must have to be a good developer. Math, physics, and chemistry are all going to help teach you this skill so apply yourself to these areas and that work will pay off. Although computer science and computer skills are more commonly being offered as an option at high school, it isn't a requirement for aspiring developers and many successful developers now in the industry did not have this as an option in high school. I had done plenty of website creation and JavaScript but had never used a compiled language until I reached college. To be honest, it didn't slow me down too much, but if your high school offers any computer science or programming courses, you might as well start early. If they don't, you should still try to get some exposure on your own through online courses or just by trying to do it yourself. If you build a mobile app or website while still in high school you are going to be well prepared for the future.

Getting a job, even if it has nothing to do with computer science, is probably a good idea for many high school students. The developers I've known who never worked before their career usually lack some determination and professionalism. The money in a high school job probably won't be good and the work will probably be menial, but that's kind of the point. You will appreciate your first job writing code way more if you, like me, have spent a summer doing something like stocking shelves overnight at a grocery store.

Navigating Through University

There are hundreds of books written about getting into university and I'm not an expert in this area, so if you are approaching the time in life to start considering college applications then you and your family are going to have to become knowledgeable in this area. The problem solving you prepared for in high school is going to help your standardized test scores and hopefully your interest in learning will make you the kind of student universities are looking for.

The kind of university you get into will certainly play a large part in your first job but it isn't an all-or-nothing proposition. There is a demand for software developers from all schools (and even those without formal training), but the tech companies I've worked at see universities in three general buckets:

1. Top computer science schools - If you are in a top CS school, you are almost always going to be able to get at least a first interview at any tech company. This list includes the names you've heard of - Stanford, Caltech, Berkeley, MIT, Carnegie Mellon, University of Washington, UT Austin, Georgia Tech, etc. If you make it into one of these schools, congratulations! Don't mess up this opportunity and you will have not only lined yourself up for all the interviews you want, but you'll have an advantage in future promotions and opportunities based on your school name alone.

2. Well-respected schools - While your education is going to depend as much on you as it does on the school you get into, there is a hierarchy of school reputations and not every school is top tier. If you made it into a well-respected but not-top tier school you are still in competition for spots at top tier tech companies, but you'll have to do a little bit more to stand out. See the sections on resumes and interviewing for more, but

make sure that you are doing the kinds of activities in college that make you stand out and make sure you make full use of career fairs and other networking events. Tech companies of all sizes make tons of hires from these types of schools (often large state schools or great private universities) but the competition is going to be a bit stiffer. I went to a great but not top school and although the most selective employers like Google were not on campus, I know of many alumni from my university who are there now and at other extremely selective employers. There aren't any limits to your achievement if you go to a school like this, but you are going to have to deliver more on your own and rely less on the reputation of your alma mater.

3. The rest - About a quarter of the people I work with did not come from any of the top or most respected schools but managed to find ways to work their way to the top. Top tech companies will not be heavily recruiting directly from these schools, but they will still look at resumes and pick out the best students. It sounds harsh, but at Amazon these schools were often used as 'filler,' recruited from later in the year when the company knew what the yield was from the schools in (1) and (2). Employers are going to be more selective so you really have to stand out as one of the top candidates from your school. If you don't manage to get a top job straight out of school and that is your goal, don't despair. The people I work with who followed this path started at local or regional tech companies, excelled there, and then were hired by top tech companies.

Majors and Minors
If you're interested in working in software development (and if you're reading this book then I hope you are) then your top goal in school

should be getting a Bachelor of Science in Computer Science. Computer Science is the preferred or required degree for almost all software development positions; if you want the best chance of employment and highest compensation, this is the degree to get. That being said, I have worked with a number of successful software engineers with other hard-science degrees like computer engineering, math, or physics, but those are the exception. Business-oriented degrees like Information Technology and Information Systems have their place in the world, but if your passion is software development you are going to have a much harder time getting a development job with one of those degrees.

A minor is nice to have but should be balanced against doing well in your major and any part-time work that you do. Many computer science curricula require a lot of math and science courses so it is natural for many to do the small set of additional courses and get a math or physics minor. English, business, and linguistics are other minors that can complement a CS major nicely and help you develop a little more well-rounded perspective.

Making the Most of Part-Time Employment

For many students, getting part-time employment while at school is a necessity, not a choice, but even if it isn't, I've seen a number of benefits to developers. There are a surprising number of jobs on campus now that can give you the kinds of experiences you want on your resume and that you can talk about in an interview. Most departments will hire a group of students to maintain web servers or build software for courses. These are great opportunities to get some programming experience that is closer to the real world. The most ideal position to take will probably be as a research assistant to a professor in the computer science department. Acting as a research assistant usually pays decently, will give you awareness of a CS specialization, and will give you a professor who can act as a reference in case you decide to go to graduate school. Even if you don't get a job doing software development in school, the rigors and responsibilities of an on-campus job will probably help your work ethic, and the money doesn't hurt either.

Securing an Internship

Getting an internship is absolutely critical in lining up your career in software development. I can't think of anyone I've worked with who graduated in the last 5 years and didn't have an internship somewhere. Getting an internship will 1) Give you the first of hopefully many job offers provided you do well, 2) Give you great material for your resume and for interviews, and 3) Give you some experience and maturity that will make you more prepared for your final year(s) in school and the beginning of your career.

Your ideal target for an internship will be a company you have your eye on working for, but don't put all your eggs in one basket. There are plenty of other companies that may not be your dream job but still have extensive software internship programs that are worth falling back on if you don't get your top choice (think Wal-Mart's website or information systems division). Take finding an internship just as seriously as you would finding your first real job because for many, one will lead to the other.

The later sections on resumes and interviewing will give you an idea of how to get attention and how to impress. but put in the time to prepare even if you are a long way from graduation. You might as well start trying to get an internship even after your first year. You probably won't get an offer but you'll get plenty of interview and career-fair experience that will better your odds for the next year and the critical final year.

The Graduate School Decision

Deciding whether to go to graduate school for a master's degree or Ph.D. is going to be a very personal choice. At the tech companies I've worked with, I've seen about a 50/50 split between those with and without advanced degrees, so you can be successful either way you choose. The value an employer places on the degree you hold is going to vary wildly, but here are some observations from my work in West Coast tech companies:

- Starting salaries are going to be a bit higher for Master's degree holders. For college hires, there was around a $5000 premium (~6%) for new grads with master's degrees.
- Some positions strongly favor those with master's degrees. This is mainly in areas with a research component like research scientists or machine learning engineers.
- Having a master's degree will open up options outside the core work of software engineering, such as teaching.
- Although many engineers have plans to return to school to pursue a master's degree, very few actually do.
- I have not seen a difference in the speed or likelihood of promotion based on degree.
- After a couple of years, compensation depends far more on individual performance and the degree pay difference will mostly be gone.
- I have not seen much difference in interview success rates between master's and bachelor's degree holders. If anything, for new graduates, the success rates for bachelor's degree holders is a little bit higher, likely because many of the CS fundamentals are fresh in mind.
- The two years spent pursuing a master's degree are two fewer years earning income, which even for fresh graduates is pretty high.

Whichever path you choose to pursue, your own talent and delivery of results will matter far more in the long run than which degree you choose. I don't think it is worth it to go into debt for a master's and then pursue software development, but if the degree will be fully paid for (ideally with a stipend as well), then it is more of an even call.

Getting Attention: Steps to a Great Resume

In 8+ years of hiring and interviewing, I've looked through thousands of resumes. any of them are terrible. You don't need to knock it out of the park with a super-stylized sales person's resume, but you do have to understand the purposes for a resume and then not commit any grave mistakes. To start, you should understand that your resume is going to serve two purposes and those two purposes can have some subtle contradictions.

The first purpose of the resume is to just get the attention of the recruiter in order to get into their pipeline. What makes resumes work well here is similar to search engine optimization - you have to understand the types of skills and technologies that they are looking for and make sure that they are contained and easy to read in your resume. Having a block of certifications and skills near the top makes it easy for recruiters to see that you meet the basic requirements of the job they are trying to match. Calling out your degree clearly can also help, as will any clearances (e.g. Top Secret) and certifications that may be required for a job.

The second purpose of the resume is to prepare the discussion for your interviews and serve as talking points. This is where a bit of narrative on your accomplishments in your previous positions comes in. By calling out some of the highlights of the work you have done and their results, you set yourself up well to explain the how and why in your interview. Another great talking point is"extracurriculars," things you have done outside your job. If you are a contributor to an open source project or have built an app on your own, you absolutely should include it in your resume. Your interviewers will definitely notice.

If you aren't careful in tailoring your resume to this second purpose (as an interview jumping-off point) then your resume will actually work against you in an interview. This is why it is critical to not put technologies or skills on your resume unless you can back them up to some degree. Unless you wrote the book on effective Java, calling yourself a 10/10 expert in Java is just asking for the interviewer to try to find questions to stump you. If you last used the skill in university ten years ago, there is no place for it on your resume.

In my review of many resumes, here are the sections for your resume that make for the cleanest accomplishment of these purposes

1. Header - Name, phone number, email address. Most companies will have no need for a physical address until later in the process so skip it.

2. Objective - Include an objective if your resume doesn't quite match what you want to do or if you aren't open to general software development. If you want to do machine learning or have a strong preference, it's fine to include it. If you don't really care or are just coming out of college, it's going to sound generic and lame so drop it.

3. Skills - Only include what is going to be relevant to your position and what you actually could talk about without sounding clueless. You can include scripting languages, compiled language, markup languages, Unix variants, source repositories you have worked with, certifications you have achieved, and so on.

4. Experience - In one to two sentences, write in your own words what your company is and what your team does in the company. Then, in a short paragraph describe your role and some of your accomplishments. This must be done in a way that another technical person who has no familiarity with your company (and often your industry) can understand. If you have been in a position for a couple of years, breaking out a

couple of projects that you have worked on makes for great openings in an interview, but keep each one brief.

5. Education - Only include high school if you have a spectacular reason to. Otherwise, just stick with your college degree and minor, GPA if well over 3.0, and any extracurricular activities.

6. Awards and contributions - If you have patents or published papers, include those in your resume unless you worked at a patent mill and have a huge number that you wouldn't be able to describe. You should also include your contributions to open source and other projects that you do outside of work. In my experience, outside interests and contributions are one of the strongest predictors of interview success. Outside contributions are a great sign of passion for our craft and can make great talking points for your interview.

It might be useful to some to see what this ends up looking like put together. Since it is going to look different depending on where you are in your career path, I've included a sample resume for a college candidate and one for a more seasoned developer.

Sample College Resume

A Turing
555.555.5555
turing@gmail.com

Technical Skills

Programming: Java, Spring, Hibernate, C/C++, Ruby.
Database: Oracle, MySQL, MongoDB.
Scripting: Perl, shell scripting.
Development Tools and Environments: Linux, Ubuntu, Git, Subversion, Perforce, Eclipse, IntelliJ
Testing: JUnit, Easymock, Cobertura, Selenium.

Experience

Research Assistant, Online Accessibility Lab, University of America, August 2013 - Present.
In the Online Accessibility Lab, I work with graduate and undergraduate students under the direction of faculty to research web and accessibility standards. My primary work has been to build a web scraping tool that scores websites based on their compliance with a set of accessibility standards. I used Java with jsoup to parse and score the websites and store that result in a MySQL database that is used by other researchers for analysis. In the last 6 months, we have scraped 20,000 websites and I have maintained and updated the tool as our project scales.

Software Development Intern, Widget Team, Awesome Blogs Inc., June 2015 - August 2015.
Awesome Blogs is a blogging platform that allows individuals and companies to build fast and beautiful blogs. On the widget team, I built a visitor counter widget that highlighted the number of visits to a

blog. I used Java and JSTL with jQuery backed by a NoSQL database to build this scalable and customizable widget for blog authors. My widget was installed more than 2000 times in the first week after it launched.

Interests and Awards
- Eastwood High Valedictorian.
- 2 years on Dean's list.
- 2014 Newton scholarship recipient.
- Frequent contributor to jsoup, an open source Java web parser library. The accessibility filter layer in jsoup was primarily my contribution and is now part of the master branch (include a Github link).

Sample Industry Resume

A Turing
555.555.5555
turing@gmail.com

Technical Skills

Programming: I have 8 years experience with Java within J2EE (Oracle Application Server, IBM Websphere Application Server) as well as lightweight Java utilizing Spring, Hibernate, and the JSTL. I have 4 years experience working with Ruby and web scripting in Perl and Python.

Database: I have built on and optimized for Oracle, MySQL, MongoDB.

Development Tools and Environments: Linux, Ubuntu, Git, Subversion, Perforce, Eclipse, IntelliJ

Testing: JUnit, Easymock, Cobertura, Selenium.

Experience

Senior Software Development Engineer, Core Application Team, Awesome Blogs Inc, 2012 - Present.

Awesome Blogs is a blogging platform that allows individuals and companies to build fast and beautiful blogs. The core application team owns the evolution and operations of the core blogging platform, including hosting, security, and performance. As a senior engineer, I do architecture, design, implementation, consultation, and mentoring for engineers on my team and across the company. Accomplishments include:

- Migration of infrastructure from dedicated rack space to Amazon Web Services, saving our company $200,000 annually on infrastructure.
- Re-architecture of core blogging framework which raised availability from 99.75% to 99.989%.

23

- Security assessment and response plans to high severity issues related to OpenSSL, Bash shell, Cross Site Request Forgery and Cross Site Scripting.
- Organizer of and regular presenter at the Awesome Blogs Engineering Brownbag, a forum for informal presentations on technical trends and engineering accomplishments.

Software Development Engineer, Widget Team, Awesome Blogs Inc., 2008 - 2012.
As a member of the widget team, I designed, built, and maintained widgets to be used by blog authors. Some of my work included:

- Designed and implemented a cross-blog chat system in use by over 10,000 blogs and reaching peak messages per second of 1000. Built in Ruby and the chat history persisted with MongoDB.
- Implemented a social-media addition widget that is now standard across all new Awesome Blog templates. The social-media addition widget is purely client side and built using jQuery with HTML5 and responsive CSS.
- Consistently the top resolver of customer defects during my rotations as the on-call engineer.

Research Assistant, Online Accessibility Lab, University of America, 2007 - 2008.
In my university's Online Accessibility Lab, I worked with graduate and undergraduate students under the direction of faculty to research web and accessibility standards. My primary work was to build a web scraping tool that scores websites based on their compliance with a set of accessibility standards. I used Java with jsoup to parse and score the websites and store that result in a MySQL database that was used by other researchers for analysis. In the last 6 months of this job, we scraped 20,000 websites and I maintained and updated the tool as it scaled.

Software Development Intern, Widget Team, Awesome Blogs Inc., June 2007 - August 2007.

On the widget team at Awesome Blogs, I built a visitor counter widget that highlighted the number of visits to a blog. I used Java and JSTL with jQuery backed by a NoSQL database to build this scalable and customizable widget for blog authors. My widget was installed more than 2000 times in the first week after it launched.

Interests and Awards

- Primary Contributor on US Patent #57668541 - System for determining artificial or human intelligence.
- Contributor on US Patent #55985581 - System for binary encoding and decoding.
- Lead developer for jTuring, an open source application for artificial intelligence.
- 4 year Top-Tier (top 10% of the organization) rating at AwesomeBlogs

Things to Avoid

Your resume, of course, doesn't have to look anything like these samples to be taken seriously, but remember to be precise, concise, and structured. Make it easy to read both for interviewers as well as for recruiters who will just be giving it a quick glance. Remember to include outside interests and accomplishments to make you stand out from everyone else at your company.

As you are putting together your resume, there are plenty of things to avoid. Some of the top resume mistakes I see that you should watch for in your own resume are:

1. Too long - If you are graduating from college, you get one page. That's all. If you have a couple years of industry experience you get two pages. Anything beyond that and you had better be interviewing for a very senior level position (and probably don't need this book).

2. Company Descriptions copied verbatim - While I may still consider your resume, if you have the full mission statement paragraph from your company copied into your resume you are going to start off in the hole with me. I have had candidates include copied mission statements for every one of the companies they had taken a contract with, 8 in all. Needless to say, that resume went to the (digital) shredder. If you don't understand well enough what your company does and what your role in the company is, you aren't going to convince anyone that you'll understand their needs any better.

3. Unsubstantiated Skills - Having to answer, "I've only read about it" or "I just learned about it in college" to a question about something in your resume is, in my book, an instant fail

to an interview. Don't put it on your resume if you can't back it up.

4. Worthless Skills - If you still have on your resume that you are competent in Windows 98 and 2000 you are badly in need of a resume makeover.

5. Typos - Your resume must be proofread, preferably by one person who is technical and one person who is not.

6. Inappropriate or lame email addresses - Just get a Gmail address that is close to your name and be done with it. If you are using an email you thought was cool in high school or the email address of your internet service provider, those are going to be marks against you, even if those marks may be unconscious..

7. Acronyms - This seems to happen most with resumes I've seen from healthcare or government contractors. If you are applying for my job then I am your audience and I should not be expected to try to decipher your coded work descriptions.

8. Worthless information - We know we can get references by request, so there is no need to state that (or to write out your references right in your resume). Further, if your objective is generic (I want a position where I can solve problems working in a fast-paced environment…), just drop it.

9. Too Generic - Just saying what your company does isn't enough. Tell me what you did that helped the company. I should be able to envision you doing that for my team.

10. Too Dense - Since there isn't anyone (not the recruiter, not your interviewer) who really wants to spend time poring over

your resume, make it easy to digest. Use bullet points, be concise, and understand what we want to hear.

By putting together a solid resume, you will open doors with recruiters and set the tone for positive and engaging interviews.

First Contact: Getting Your Resume to a Hiring Manager

Once your resume is polished you are ready to start trying to get it in front of a hiring manager and get some interviews set up. For most large companies, there are 2 different kinds of recruiting organizations. There is the college recruiting department which deals with students and campuses to bring in interns and new college grads. From the giant pool of applications and the giant set of teams that have a need, the college recruiting department will try to match based on preference and need. As a college candidate, there is a decent chance that the people you interview with are not going to be the team you work with, and the team you work with could even change between the time you interview and the time you join, depending on the team's needs. For industry candidates, you should be applying for specific positions and will work with recruiting teams that are focused on meeting a single organization's needs. Making a relationship with the recruiter and the hiring manager matters far more for you than for college candidates as the team that sees your resume, interviews you, and works with you are all the same. There are a couple of different avenues to getting attention at a large company. Which one you use will depend on your network and where you are in your career path.

Employee Referral

For both candidates and companies, employee referrals are the best way to make an entry into the system. In fact, most companies are so encouraging of this that they will often offer significant bounties to employees who get their friends and contacts to join. If you are still in school, the most useful contacts in your network will probably be family friends in the industry or older classmates who are now employed.

If you are in school, try to ensure that your contact in the company not only submits your referral to the general college or internship pipeline but that they make contact with someone in college recruiting as well.

College recruiting departments for major tech companies receive tens of thousands of resumes and hundreds of referrals; you want to make sure yours gets seen.

For industry hires, rather than just working through the recruiter, have your inside referrer make contact with the hiring manager first and talk you up. Once that's been done, your referrer can get your resume through to their recruiting group through the normal channels. With the candidate already on the hiring manager's mind (and your contact should let the recruiter know that), your chances of getting an interview should be close to guaranteed if your skills are at all a match.

LinkedIn Networking

LinkedIn has been a major help for job finders and recruiters alike. As a job seeker (or potential job seeker), there are two ways to approach using LinkedIn to get in front of recruiters and hiring managers. The first way is the passive approach. By continually broadening your network and accepting connections from recruiters (who move around a lot between companies), you are going to be on their radar when they do job searches with keywords that match your LinkedIn profile. For this to work, your profile has to be complete (including resume, current job, skills, etc.) but is far less effort when recruiters come to you. When I was working at Amazon as a developer, even with a pretty minimal profile (and 200+ connections), I would get contacted a couple times a week from recruiters locally and nationally. Tend to your network and it will be a solid resource for new opportunities.

The second way to use LinkedIn is by using it more aggressively to contact recruiters for companies you are interested in. While you might think it is most natural to reach out directly to the manager you anticipate working for, they will probably be put off by your random requests. Recruiters, on the other hand, are constantly under pressure to hit monthly goals and so any request that comes to them directly is one that they don't have to find by spamming dozens of random people. Just a simple search for 'recruiter *company*' will likely turn up a couple of names. Don't start reaching out to too many, as companies will have a system to avoid duplicate entries. Pick one recruiter and try to connect by letting them know you are interested in learning more about positions at the company. If they don't answer, feel free to move on to the next. Do be aware that often recruiters at large companies can share LinkedIn notes with each other about candidates (to avoid overloading the same candidate from different recruiters), so if you make a connection with one, avoid trying to start conversations with other recruiters from the same company, at least over LinkedIn.

Direct Submission

If you don't know anyone within the organization or company you want, and you can't make contact with the recruiter over LinkedIn, then your last direct resort is a submission through the company's normal jobs site. When you make a direct submission, don't just blindly send a resume to the company's careers email address. Those are overloaded and flooded with spam. Instead, look through the careers page to find specific jobs that are available. Avoid the general descriptions that were probably written for a large organization and instead look for descriptions that look like they were written for a specific team. Apply to 2 or 3 of them at most and then wait for a response. If you don't hear back within a week, you can apply to another position, but give recruiters at least a couple days to see your resume, check with the hiring manager if they want to move forward, and get back to you.

Job Hunting Sites

LinkedIn has become the primary passive recruiting tool for most job finders in tech, but sites like Monster, Dice, Indeed, and CareerBuilder are all sites that tech recruiters will pore over. Keeping your resume up-to-date here won't hurt (unless you don't want your current company knowing), but the other paths are probably going to be more fruitful.

College Career Fair

For college candidates, if you don't have a strong referral, the best opening to getting an interview is going to be your college career fair. If the company you are targeting is on your campus, it is important that you show up and make a good impression. How career fairs are handled is going to vary from company to company but at Amazon and Microsoft, the usual career fair team is one recruiting representative and 3 - 4 developers or other tech employees who will chat with candidates and do some initial screening. The initial screening consists of a quick (10 second) resume review, a question or two about your interests, and maybe a small problem-solving question. Depending on how the candidate does, at Amazon we assigned a 1-5 ranking. A ranking of 5 means that they must interview this candidate, a 4 is a strong recommendation, a 3 means only interview if there is room, and a 1 to 2 means there were significant gaps in skills, communication issues, or the wrong kind of degree. From those rankings, Amazon would then set up interviews either on campus, over the phone, or by flying candidates to headquarters in Seattle. Since so many hires come from career fairs, it is important to make the right impression. I've worked in 4-5 career fairs as a representative and went numerous times as a student. Some of the things I learned were:

1) Go when there aren't a ton of candidates - At all of the career fairs I've attended, the first thirty minutes were mostly empty. The employers you are talking to first thing in the morning are going to be less stressed and more hungry to start finding candidates. You're also going to have to spend less time waiting in lines and are going to have a quieter atmosphere to hear and think through the questions you are asked.

2) Be prepared to answer some basic background questions - You need to have an answer for what your interests are and why you want to work at the companies you are applying to. Try to tie your interest to

something you have already achieved, like an open source project or research work. That is going to make you stand out from everyone else who has a generic interest in technology but hasn't backed it up in any substantial way.

3) Be prepared to do small problem solving - Most of the questions you will be asked to solve on the spot will be as simple as just using the right data structure for a given problem. Have a surface-level knowledge (run-time, space usage, etc.) of all the standard data structures as well as a deeper understanding of sorting, data structure traversal, etc. You should be able to explain a quicksort for an array or a depth-first or breadth-first traversal of a tree without any hesitation.

4) Bring a pen - If you're asked to do any small problem solving, you may want to take notes or sketch a diagram, so bring your own pen (or one you pick up from another booth!).

5) Dress appropriately - If you are applying to a West Coast tech company (Amazon, Microsoft, Google, Adobe, Netflix, Apple, etc.), then there is no need to dress up in a suit. You should wear what you always wear to school. (This is definitely true if you move on to interviews. do not show up to an interview with one of these companies in anything formal.) If you are looking at finance or more traditional companies then you may have to dress up more. Wearing a suit is uncomfortable, but put up with it for an afternoon to fit the image they are expecting.

6) Go to company info sessions - In addition to attending career fairs, you should also go to any other events being held by interesting companies on campus. Whether a company is there for the career fair or just for a one-off visit, it is a good chance for you to learn more about the company (and have better material for questions to ask in interviews) as well as a chance to get your resume out. As if that wasn't enough, they just about always have pizza and free swag.

College Jobs Site

If the company of your choice doesn't come to your campus career fair, you'll have to go to them. One way that campuses pull resumes is by working with college job sites. These make it easy for companies to regionalize their efforts and contact the best looking resumes from a given school for interviews. If your college doesn't have a common careers site or there aren't many employers listed, you'll have to reach out directly to the company through email or LinkedIn.

Getting In the Door: What to Expect In Interviews

Once your resume has gotten the attention of recruiting and hiring managers then the next phase of the process begins:it is time for interviews. The number and interval of interviews is going to depend on the type of position as well as the circumstances of the event or the department you are talking with. Some formats I've seen across Amazon and Microsoft are:

1. Internships - 2 phone screens and then a decision.
2. Internships - 2 in-person interviews and then a decision.
3. Internships - 2 in-person interviews, then a decision, then if positive a final interview and a decision.
4. Full time - 4 in-person interviews either on campus (college candidates) or at a hotel or events center (industry hires).
5. Full time - Online assessment (a 1-2 hour set of problems online) then, if positive, 4 - 5 in-person interviews.
6. Full time - 1-2 phone interviews then, if positive, 4-5 in-person interviews.

There are many different formats, even beyond these 6, but the point is that even for an internship you are going to be talking with multiple people coming from different perspectives, though most of them will play by the same broad script. Most large tech companies use a mixture of problem-solving coding/design questions to assess your technical ability and behavioral questions to determine your culture and leadership fit. We'll cover more on these two types of question in later chapters, but there are some general tips to keep in mind as you prepare for and participate in tech interviews:

1. Be enthusiastic - I have seen many cases where a candidate on the edge was tipped one way or the other based on their enthusiasm level. Whether this comes natural to you or you have to fake it, you need to sound passionate about the work

that you are doing and passionate about the opportunity that is presenting itself. I once was on an interview loop for a developer who wrote code to analyze and report when senior care center patients needed new bed-linens and undergarments. The candidate was sound technically, but what our interview team couldn't stop talking about was, "if this candidate, who has literally the crappiest job we have ever heard of, is this excited now, just wait to see how he would be at our company!" If you aren't naturally enthusiastic, try practicing to a tape recorder or friends and family until you can at least fake it for a day. (Most engineers aren't extremely enthusiastic by nature, and it isn't mandatory to passing an interview, but it sure helps)

2. Be rested - If you are travelling for an interview, don't make it a super-hero trip where you take the red-eye, sleep for a couple hours, then show up thinking you are going to be fine. For locals, still make sure you get a good night' sleep even if it means taking some melatonin or a sleep aid to calm down. Throughout the day, keep your energy and attention high by having coffee, juice or other drinks.

3. Take advantage of offered breaks - Every interviewer should be offering you a chance to get a drink or use the restroom between interviews. If they do not, feel free to ask for it.

4. Do not complain about your current or previous employers. Ever.

5. Do not talk to interviewers or recruiters about compensation. That happens after you get the offer.

6. Don't assume any time is off the record. Even if it is a lunch conversation or a recruiter from HR, don't let your guard down

over a meal and don't push the recruiter with questions you wouldn't feel comfortable asking any other interviewers. You don't know the dynamics of the decision group so don't run any risks of turning someone off.

7. Don't wear a suit to interview at a West Coast tech company. Don't neglect to wear a suit if you are interviewing with Morgan Stanley. Ask the recruiter what to wear and actually follow their advice.

8. Be careful knowing too much about your interviewers' background. Your recruiting contact may provide you the names of your interviewers in advance and it is going to be very natural to Google them or look at them on LinkedIn. That's fine but be careful what you do with that information. If someone is a leader in their field or you really do have some kind of common interest, it is fine to mention that you were looking at the background of your interviewers and saw this connection. What's less appropriate is when your question isn't based on a common connection and is just an arbitrary shot in the dark because you read the advice somewhere to study the background of your interviewers. I once had a candidate asked about a random project I had worked on that was on my LinkedIn profile, but because they did it with no explanation and the project itself wasn't very noteworthy, it caught me off-guard, which is never something you want to do to an interviewer.

With some of these tips in mind, let's focus now on the meat of the interviews and the two types of questions you are going to get.

Acing the Interview: Behavioral Questions

Traditional interviews leave a lot of open-ended questions and look for your broad opinions on topics. Interview prompts like "What are your strengths?" and "Tell me about yourself" and "What do you bring to our company?" can lead to very scripted and canned answers that don't actually tell a lot about your experience and make it hard to understand how you will behave in the future. Behavioral interviews are there to probe for specific instances in your experience where you have been faced with a situation, and then dive into how you responded and what the outcome was.

To prepare for behavioral interviews, you need to understand the company culture and leadership principles, prepare your own set of experiences from your past, and then structure your response.

Understand the Company and Leadership Principles
How you orient your answers and build up your set of examples is going to depend on the culture of the company that you want to work for. If you want to work at Apple, getting something out quick and dirty with future time to iterate isn't going to be the approach to take. If you want to work at Microsoft, stressing open standards and open data is probably also not the optimal trait (though they are getting a lot better). While some companies make it very easy to see the leadership principles they look for (just searching online for Amazon Leadership Principles will take you to a page on their website which calls out exactly what they want), for others the best way to learn will be by talking to friends or contacts who work there. Offer to buy a cup of coffee or lunch for someone currently employed there and get their insight into what the company values.

Prepare Your Experiences

Even though you make decisions every day, when you are put on the spot to come up with an example of a certain kind of experience your mind may go blank if you haven't prepared. Just answering that you "do that a lot but can't think of a specific answer"or really any other answer that is a non-answer is going to get you negative marks in an interview. Further, trying to lie your way through an experience is not likely to go well for you (remember, you may only interview once every couple of years but many interviewers will be interviewing a hundred candidates a year) so spend the time up front examining your past so you don't have to try to make things up on the spot.

To prepare for these questions, you should think back to the last couple of years and come up with a list of situations where you had to make decisions. Focus on some of the following areas and come up with one or two examples of times when you were in these situations:

Technical Background
On your technical background, they will be looking to assess your ability to problem solve through design and coding, which we will cover more in the Technical Questions section. Companies will also want to see your ability to invent, to improve the environment in which you work, and your passion for technology. Think about situations you could use to answer prompts like:

- Tell me about the most innovative thing you have done. What were the results?
- Tell me about a time when the normal way of doing things would not work. What did you do differently?
- Tell me about an improvement you have made to a team's development, testing, or deployment process.
- Tell me about something you are working on or learning about outside your core responsibilities (can be either at work or at home).
- Tell me about a new technology or design pattern that you've applied.

Project Delivery

Employers want to measure your ability to deliver projects. How hard will you push? What tradeoffs will you make? How much do you understand and care about the customer? The balance each company looks for will be different but you can expect discussions around your work with projects and customers like:

- Tell me about a project that looked impossible but you delivered it anyway. How did you do it?
- Tell me about a time when you had to dive into a project without a complete set of information (design, requirements, etc.). How did you proceed?
- How do you know when a project is complete?
- How do you prioritize different tasks in your day (code reviews, designs, coding, etc.)?

Working with a Team

Most of the software you write will be as part of a team. Finding someone who can work well with a team is often even more important than finding someone who is amazing technically. Your interviewers will want to see that you know when to disagree but also know when to back down. They will want to see that you raise up others on the team and improve overall efficiency. You will get prompts like:

- Tell me about a time when you disagreed with your manager. What was it and how did you resolve it?
- Tell me about a time when you disagreed with a peer or project owner, how did you address it?
- Tell me about a time when you disagreed but ultimately lost the argument. How did you proceed?
- Tell me about the effect you have had on helping another individual progress.
- How do you raise the morale or effectiveness of new teams?
- How do you establish trust when joining a new team?

Self-Awareness

You need to be humble and self-aware enough to recognize that you have weaknesses but that you also learn from mistakes. This is not the time to reveal that you twice broke the whole website for your previous company, or spill all your biggest fears and overblow your problems. You should, however, be aware that you aren't perfect but you are improving. Some prompts can include:

- Tell me about a mistake in judgment you made. What led to that decision?
- Tell me about a mistake you have made but were able to apply that learning in the future.
- What do you do to ramp up on a new team?
- How do you know when to keep trying to solve a problem on your own and when to reach out to others?

Structuring Your Response

Once you have studied the types of behaviors the company is looking for and have a set of situations from your past at the ready, you just need to structure your response correctly.

When you structure your response, the simplest way to organize your thoughts in a way the interviewer wants to hear is the Situation-Behavior-Impact model. First, briefly describe the situation. Don't go through the full history of the company or every nuance of the project. Stick with what is going to be relevant to the story you are telling. Be sure not to simplify it so much, or to be so thick with company- or industry-specific language, that your interviewer can't easily follow or visualize the situation.

Second, describe the behavior you took. This isn't a time to talk about the team effort or fill your explanation with "we." The interviewer is looking for what *you* specifically did in the situation. This isn't limited just to the actions taken but can include what you were thinking and why you acted the way you did.

Lastly, describe the effects of your actions. If they aren't confidential, knowing some of the hard numbers involved (in performance improvements, user impressions, contacts reduced, revenue increases, etc.) will give your story more color, but interviewers will also understand if you can only speak in percentages. Demonstrate that you are aware of the results not just on the technical pieces of the system but also on the benefits to customers.

Let's take an example. Suppose the question was, "How do you establish trust when joining a new team?" An answer might be, "When I joined the widget team at Awesome Blogs, I wanted to demonstrate my willingness to dive into the system and to establish trust in the team. I saw early on that there was a pile of operational issues to investigate--cases where customers were reporting missing comments on their blogs. The other members on my team were concerned but were all focused on their own projects and didn't have time to dive in. Because my ramp-up task was going faster than planned, I took the extra time I had and some time at night to add additional logging around our comment submission system with the hope of uncovering what the root cause was. Just a logging change had little risk and my team signed off on the change without issue. Once my change was out, I was able to use that new information to identify a race condition in storing comments which I was able to work with a more senior engineer to fix. With the fix in place, our customers were happy and my teammates saw I was willing to get in and get to work."

Talking yourself up is not something you normally do outside of performance reviews and interviews, so practice a little bit and be ready. By understanding company values, keeping a bank of experiences, and cleanly structuring your responses, you'll demonstrate to the interviewer that you are someone who is going to make their team and company stronger.

Acing the Interview: Technical Questions

While the behavioral and culture fit portions of interviews are important and you won't be hired if you don't impress there, for software developers the majority of interview time is spent answering technical questions. The types of questions you are asked can be diverse and can range from bits and bytes through to scripting, internet protocols to database theory, coding, problem solving, and designing objects and systems. Before we look at the range of questions and some sample questions and answers, there are some things to keep in mind throughout this portion of your interview.

1) There are some things you just need to know - Things like how powers of 2 work, how to determine the running time of an algorithm, CS fundamentals, are all things you have to know in advance.

2) There is much more that you aren't expected to know - I have had a surprising number of candidates who, when presented with a creative problem, answer something along the lines of "I'm not sure, I haven't solved this problem before." I have to restrain myself from smacking my head, and as far as I can remember, nobody who has answered that way to me has ever been hired. None of the larger problems we ask you are ones we expect you to have solved before. We are looking for your ability to solve new and unfamiliar problems because that is what we do every day.

3) Understand the problem before you dive in - It's an immediate warning sign when candidates just dive into a problem without asking any clarifying questions. Most of the questions asked are intentionally ambiguous. Don't dive in until you understand the boundaries of the problem and know that you are solving the right cases.

4) Speak your thoughts - Even if you are going to be brilliant and nail the problem without hesitation, you're still expected to talk us through your solution, preferably before you actually get to code. Talk to us about what tradeoffs you are considering and why you are making decisions.

5) Use the whiteboard - There will be either paper or a whiteboard; make extensive use of it. You want the interviewer to understand your solution, and for most design and coding questions, the whiteboard is the best way to go.

6) Don't just stop - If you get stuck, take a step back and rethink the problem. If that isn't getting you anywhere, explain what is getting you stuck. Alternatively, if you think you are done, don't just stand around, explain why you think the problem is solved and ask the interviewer if they want further explanation on an area. You should also be sure to go back and verify your work, describe test cases, and make sure you are meeting the expectations of the problem.

The exact questions you get are going to be impossible to predict, but there are a number of different categories of questions that you might encounter so it will be helpful to see some examples of these in order to understand what the interviewer is looking for. This short book is not going to be able to give you a complete course in computer science, algorithms, or data structures; you are going to have to learn those on your own (see the selected readings at the end for starters). But these example questions can help guide your further preparation. All of these questions I've either asked or seen others ask, so take the time to study and prepare your answers for topics like these.

CS Fundamentals
You need to know not just the practical side of programming, you'll need to know CS theory as well. This means understanding things like run-time and space complexity (Big-O), memory allocation (stack vs

heap), object oriented design principles (encapsulation, inheritance, and polymorphism), as well as data structures and algorithms (more on those later).

Data Structures

You need to know about a variety of data structures both in theory (run-time to add, lookup, etc.) as well as in practice (when and how to use). Not only are data structures often a category of questions on their own, they are often the foundation for getting any of the algorithms right. Some of the types of questions to have down cold are:

- What are the qualities and differences of arrays, linked lists, stacks, queues? (Know what they are and how to implement.)
- What is a binary search tree, a trie, or a red/black tree?
- What is a b-tree?
- What is a heap? Min-heap? Max-heap?
- What is a hash table? How are they implemented? What are the characteristics of a good hashing function?

Programming Languages

You should know at least one scripting language (Perl, PHP, Ruby, Python, etc.) and one more traditional programming language (C++, Java, or C#, depending on the industry). You should know the language well enough to answer questions like:

- What is your favorite language?
- Why is it your favorite?
- What are its most powerful or interesting features?
- What is a drawback of this language?

You should also know well the syntax and keywords for this language as well as how the language is implemented.

If you are a C++ developer, you should be able to answer questions like:

- What is the difference between public, private, protected?
- What is function overloading?
- What is multiple inheritance?
- What is a pure virtual function?
- What are the differences between a struct and a class?
- What are the different primitive types? How do you decide between them?
- What is the difference between "passing by value" and "passing by reference"? What does that syntax look like?

If you are a Java developer, you should be able to answer questions like:

- What is garbage collection? What are the different ways it can be implemented?
- When would you use final, finally, finalize?
- What is the difference between StringBuilder and StringBuffer?
- How do you use threads in Java?
- How do you use an interface? Abstract class? What do those look like?
- Primitives, parameters, and objects - are they passed by reference or by value in Java? Can you change that?
- What are checked and unchecked exceptions? Give an example of each.

Whatever your language of choice, ensure that you know the set of features for that language. In addition, get an idea for how the language is actually interpreted and eventually turned into assembly instructions.

Internet Architecture
If you're interviewing for a maker of hard drives or an offline gaming company, you can skip this one. For more modern tech companies, though, a very large component of the business is web focused and there is an expectation that you don't just get on the internet, but that

you actually have some idea of how the internet works. The most common question that is asked around this (and I've seen it asked to software developers, IT folks, network engineers, web developers, software development managers as well as technical project managers) is, "When I type www.companyname.com, into my browser, what happens?". You need to be able to talk through:

- What is DNS, why is it important, how does it work? What are the different levels of caching?
- What is SSL, what is an SSL handshake?
- How does the browser and server make an initial connection (TCP SYN/SYN-ACK)?
- What are the different kinds of requests (GET/POST/etc.)? What goes with those requests (cookies, accept-encoding, user-agent, etc.)?
- What types of responses can you get back?
- What does your browser do with the content?
- What kinds of content can you get back and how do you deal with it (talk about client side features like JavaScript, CSS, etc.)?

You don't need the full knowledge of each of these steps, but you need to understand the layers involved to some degree. At Amazon, we somehow got a new college hire who didn't understand that JavaScript was purely executed on the browser and couldn't fathom why HTML comments describing business decisions were a bad thing. Needless to say, he didn't last long.

Bits and Bytes

While questions on very low-level topics are falling out of favor in some places, they are still a major part of some interviews, particularly at Google, so don't leave this as a gap in your knowledge if you have only been doing higher-level development. You need to understand:

- How to manipulate bits in the language of your choice. You should know about And, Or, Not, XOR, Bitwise shifting, etc.
- Apply bit manipulation to do things like addition and division with powers of two.

- Understand and apply bit masking.
- What is big-endian vs little-endian? (I've never actually heard of this being asked, but it takes 10 minutes to learn so it's probably worth the time.)

General Problem Solving

In addition to all the "classic" problem solving and coding that you will do, there are also some questions that require problem solving beyond just design and coding. These used to be the "brain-teaser" questions that Microsoft and Google would ask, where you would be given a silly situation or wild estimation problem so the interviewers could try to figure out how you think. Questions like that are less common now and the questions are usually of a more practical nature. One common non-coding question I've seen at both Amazon and Google is, "You get a report that the website is running slow, how do you investigate?" This question is great because it can go into many different directions and is used not just for software developers but for other positions as well. An answer from a well-rounded software developer will be able to probe into:

- All of the different metrics we would want to be gathering: everything from the database, to the server, to the client receiving the first byte, to the client receiving the last byte, to the page being fully rendered.
- Server performance and monitoring.
- Database scaling, contention, and profiling.
- Concurrency, thread starvation, algorithmic complexity, and service profiling.
- Network traffic, webpage size, and compression.
- JavaScript performance and optimal performing websites (minimize the number of separate requests, cache static assets, don't interleave JavaScript throughout the page, etc.).

Problem Solving with Coding and Algorithms

Probably the largest single area you will spend time on in an interview will be solving problems with algorithms and putting them into code on the whiteboard. Depending on what level you are interviewing for, these can range from simply applying well-known algorithms up through designing your own large-scale solutions. When you go into these problems, remember that most of them will have multiple answers, and while you will want to eventually get to the optimal one, it is almost always smart to start toat least establish the "naive" implementation. Some of the easy coding problems include:

Arrays and Strings
- Reverse a string.
- Reverse the words in a string.
- Find if a word is a palindrome.
- Determine if a string has all unique characters. Give a solution that optimizes for space and one that optimizes for time.
- Determine if one string can be formed with a subset of another $O(n \log (n))$ time).

Linked Lists
- Determine if a linked list is circular.
- Find the nth-to-last element of a linked list.
- Reverse a linked list.

Trees
- Validate a binary tree.
- Do a breadth first and depth first search.
- Determine the height of a tree.

Recursion / Iteration / Backtracking
- Implement a Fibonacci sequence with recursion, iteration, and/or memoization.
- Find the words that could make up a string literal (i.e. bed, bath, and, beyond in bedbathandbeyond).

For entry level developers, these types of data structure problem-solving questions are common. For developers with a little bit more experience, the data structure and algorithm choices are going to be more interesting. Some example questions that start scaling up are:

- Given a string, determine the average number of letters in a word, excluding punctuation.
- Determine the longest common subsequence between two strings.
- Given an integer, convert it to roman numerals.
- Given a 2d matrix representing a maze and a start and end point, find the path from start to end. Is it going to be the shortest path?
- Given the mapping of numbers to letters found on a phone keypad, convert a given sequence of numbers to the potential set of valid English words (e.g., 228 would yield 'cat', 'bat', 'act'). Be able to optimize for time or space. Understand how precomputation with a trie or hashmap would help.
- Given a 2d matrix of characters, find a given word in the matrix. Now find all English words (i.e., the game Boggle).

For all of these questions, there are going to be brute force solutions as well as solutions that use data structures or algorithms to improve on brute force. Be sure to have the conversation with the interviewer on what you are optimizing for and make sure you are solving the right problem. Also be prepared to have the same basic question wrapped in extraneous information to see if you can deal with ambiguity and cut down to the core problem. One example of this might be the question, "Given two days of log files, we want to know the set of customers that visited on both log files." I've seen this question at both Google and Amazon as part of phone interviews. The steps you might go through would be:

1. Verify that customers have some type of identifier that is in the log entries.

2. Ask about parsing the customer id. Does the interviewer want you to do that (and if so, be prepared to talk about tokenization or regular expressions), or are they really just focused on finding the intersection of two lists, a pretty straightforward problem?

3. They are probably interested in how you find the intersection (those elements in common between both) but you should verify that. You might start by saying you want to just write a naive version that you can improve on.

4. The most inefficient but simplest approach will be a for-loop inside a for-loop. In the outer for-loop, you are iterating through each entry in file 1, in the inner for-loop you are iterating through each entry in file 2.

5. Confirm that this is terrible at performance, on the order of O(n-squared).

6. Talk about optimizing for space. If you were to do an in-place sort with a quick-sort, you would only use an additional logn space and the sort would usually take O(nlogn). Once the two files are sorted, you just need to work from the beginning of each list, incrementing whichever is "smaller" (smaller based on whatever type of comparator you want to use) until one list reaches the end.

7. Now, if space is not a concern, you could mention that you could instead solve this with a runtime of O(n) by using a hashmap. Go through the first file and store all of the customers in a hashmap or hashset. Then go through the

second file and compare each customer against the hashset. If it is in, you have a match.

This type of progression shows that you can not only solve problems, but that you can also deal with ambiguity and understand tradeoffs.

Coding Style

Whether it is observed during your problem solving or whether there is an interviewer who is explicitly assigned this competency, the interview loop is going to want to get an idea of your code quality. Interviewers are looking for some of the following things:

- Variable naming.
- Encapsulation.
- Not overly complex methods.
- Testability and at least explaining the unit tests you would write.
- Comments (don't go overboard or use when not needed).
- Syntax. (This is going to vary greatly by your interviewer. Some believe that if your syntax is pretty close then an IDE will finish the gaps, while a smaller number still want you to write syntactically perfect code on a whiteboard.)

Object-Oriented Design

While there will probably be some questions on basic CS fundamentals, there will also be some questions asking you to model interactions and state by using classes. Interviewers will be looking to answer some of the following questions:

- Do you know how to identify relationships between objects (is-a vs has-a, etc.)?
- Do you understand inheritance?
- Do you understand interfaces?
- Do you know when to use design patterns and what some common ones are?
- Do you know what data types to use to represent data?
- What attributes do individual classes have?

- What methods do classes have?

Common questions I have seen in this area:
- Design a deck of cards that can be used in multiple scenarios.
- Design a parking garage.
- Design an elevator system.
- Model the game of chess.

There really aren't any quick tricks for these types of questions. Just think thoroughly about what is going to be consistent, what areas are going to change, and where your data boundaries are. When in doubt, think about how things are modeled in the real world.

System Design

If you have a couple of years' experience and are interviewing for a mid or senior position, then you are also going to have questions where you are asked to design part of or a complete system. These questions are usually pretty broad. I've seen questions like:
- Design the catalog system for Amazon.
- Design the autocomplete feature for Google search.
- Design one of the recommendation features at Amazon.
- Design the LinkedIn connections feature, including the distance-to-connection feature.
- Design a web cache. Do this for a single server as well as a fleet.
- Design a short url (like tinyurl) system.
- Design an event processor / job scheduler.

Unlike some of the basic algorithm problems, system design questions aren't meant to have cookie cutter answers; they require you to keep in mind a number of different problems. As you answer, some of the things your interviewer will be looking for are:
- Availability - Everything can fail either intentionally (datacenter failover) or unintentionally (single server or datacenter goes

down unexpectedly, network connection is severed, etc.). How do you deal with hardware and network failures in a distributed system?

- Abstraction - Be able to compartmentalize portions of your system to implement later. Understand where the interviewer wants you to focus.
- Dive deep - Abstraction is good but you also need to be able to dive deep and answer concrete questions (e.g. concretely answer how you would create unique identifiers for GUID generation).
- Concurrency - As you build, are you parallelizing and watching for deadlock and other concurrency issues?
- Real-World performance - You should at least have an order of magnitude idea of the time to fetch things from memory, a hard drive, over the network, etc. Understand what is and is not possible for a single server.
- Scaling - How do you scale horizontally? Identify the limits of a system and how to work around them.
- What needs to be synchronous? How much can you make asynchronous? What tradeoffs are there?

As you go through your discussion, remember to start by making sure you understand the question, then move to a high level architecture discussion (use the whiteboard!) and only after that is finished, start going into more of the details, keeping the topics above in mind.

Unix Knowledge

Unless you are working at Microsoft or another pure .NET shop, you should be very comfortable on the Unix command line and know the built-in toolset. You should be able to talk about grep, awk, sed, sort, uniq, top, ps, etc. You should also know when to put those to use. When you are given a problem like "You have a directory full of log files - find things that look like credit card numbers in them," that is really a trap to see if you are going to write a 100-line C program or if you just know to use grep. If you are working in a company or group that is a bit lower level, you should also understand a bit more how Unix works and have a grasp of the file system, threads/processes, memory management, and so on.

Wrapping Up

You aren't going to be able to prepare for every question and there probably will be some that stump you. If you really have your heart set on a company, or are in interview-prep mode for an internship or first job after college, you should probably spend 20-30 hours studying datastructures, algorithms, CS fundamentals, and coming up with your set of behavioral experiences. In addition to studying, the best preparation is to just take more interviews and, if you are already working at a company, give interviews yourself. When I was graduating from university, I interviewed with more than a dozen companies and I certainly was more able and competent in later interviews. Preparing based on the topics listed earlier is going to put you at an advantage over most candidates, but the odds still aren't in your favor. Amazon and Microsoft hire less than 1 in 5 who make it into in-house interviews, and odds are even less in your favor at Google and Facebook. Know that you have done all that you can to prepare, and then go in with confidence (and backup plans).

The Fun Part: Choosing an Offer and Team

After all your hard work making a clear resume, working your network to get an interview, and then prepping for and performing in the interview, you score one or more offers! Congratulations! Particularly if you got an offer at a top-tier company, once you have that name on your resume you will just about always be able to get an interview at other top-tier companies, and you really have made it. Your choice of company is going to be very personal but there are some things I've found useful to keep in mind when looking at offers.

How to Choose a Company

If you are lucky enough to have multiple offers to choose from (not too uncommon for well-prepared college grads), there are a few aspects to consider.

1. What is the trajectory of the company? While turnarounds are possible, you probably are going to have more fun and more impact with a company that is on the rise than with a company that has peaked. I had offers from a couple of teams within Hewlett-Packard early in my career and luckily passed those up. Although HP has an amazing history and still does a lot of cool things, it was (and is) struggling to define itself and in the subsequent 8 years has had numerous rounds of layoffs. Eventually the company split in two while trying to decide what their focus was.

2. What is the work/life balance? Ask this from multiple people and in multiple ways. Recognize that this varies greatly from team to team so try to get this answered by people in the team and organization you would be part of.

3. What is the compensation? More on negotiating this later, but the higher it starts, the higher future increases (in dollar terms) are going to be as well.

4. What amount of ownership will you have in the team and company? Companies with very hard lines between architecture teams, operation teams, development teams, testing teams, etc., are, to me, a lot less fun than teams where you have more ownership over what you do and what direction the team takes. This is a personal choice (maybe you want to just code in a box) but get the details on it.

5. Do people stick around?

6. Do the people you talk to seem happy?

7. Can you be passionate about the things you would build?

If this is a tough decision, get the advice of mentors, friends, and parents, but ultimately it will be your decision. My simplest advice would be to look to which company is going to open the most doors in the future. Why is that? 1) This place probably has its high reputation for a reason, and 2) If you never find that reason for a high reputation, it will be easier to move elsewhere.

How to Choose a Team

For candidates with industry experience, you probably had the job description, interview, and offer all from the same team. For college and internship candidates, you probably interviewed with a cross-section of interviewers; only after you got the offer do you get to express some preference on team. Whether it is picking a team before or after you interview, your choice of a team is almost as important as the company itself. Getting in the wrong team could slow your growth and lead to unhappiness, so it pays to take some time trying to get to know the team. Some of the things I like to look at when choosing a team are:

1. How well do I like the manager, both personally and professionally? This is the single biggest factor for most people in how much they like their job, so it pays to spend some time getting to know the manager, both through direct conversation with them as well by asking about them with members of their team or others you know in the company. Try to find a manager whose values line up with yours, whether you value promotions, work/life balance, a fun work environment, innovation, or other factors. One good indicator I've seen for finding overall good managers is during your first conversation, see how much time they spend actually trying to learn about you. If your manager is treating you just like a generic hire and the conversation is completely one-sided, that probably isn't going to change a lot when you join. If the manager is really interested in understanding you and setting up for success, that is a positive indicator.

2. How big is the team? Once a team grows beyond 8-9 developers, it will be tough to have a lot of unity and the manager is going to be stretched thin. If you prefer working solo and don't care about team cohesion, maybe this isn't important to you, but I prefer to work on smaller, focused teams.

3. How much influence does the team have on its roadmap? Does the team just take orders or does it have input on projects and priorities?

4. What is the makeup of the team? If you are a mid-level engineer and the team you are joining is filled with senior engineers, you may have a hard time making a name for

yourself or putting in changes you want. Alternatively, if you join as a new hire, having some senior talent may provide you with a number of mentors that will be useful throughout your career. Understand what you are looking for and look for a team composition that is going to be conducive to that.

Making the Most of Your Offer

There are plenty of generic career books that talk about all the creative negotiation you can do with your company and how to work for assorted benefits. In most tech companies, like any large company, there isn't actually going to be much flexibility on things like vacation days, office environment, 401k match, etc. That just leaves your salary, sign-on bonus, and stock grants.

If you are an intern or a college grad going to a large tech company you can ask about negotiating your salary, but every company I know of determines college and intern salaries purely by the degree you have.

For candidates with industry experience, you have more flexibility. Once you get an offer, you should recognize that you have now gone from being the job hunter to being the hunted. They want you, and it is important to the manager and the recruiter to now get you onboard. You would think that would mean you should ask for something way higher than what is offered, but if you ask for too much, 1) your manager may develop an immediate distrust of you or feel you are greedy, or 2) you may get what you ask for but your outsized compensation will put unreasonably high expectations on you. I would suggest asking between 5-10% more in the total compensation (salary and stock) than your initial offer. That's not greedy but is going to give you a nice boost. You should be flexible on whether that addition comes in stock, up-front bonus, or salary. There are advantages to each.

Making a Mark - Your First 90 Days

Now that you've passed the interview, chosen a company and picked a team, it's time to settle down and get to work! Your first couple of months on the job are extremely critical to making an impression on your manager and team. Don't squander this one chance to make a good first impression. As a manager, I've watched dozens of people start in new positions. From my observations, as well as the observations of others, here are the best ways to get your start.

1. Work longer and harder than anyone else during the first month. Chances are, with a new environment to get used to, you aren't going to be working smarter than anyone else in the office, but you can seize this opportunity to work the longest and hardest to make up for that. I am all about work/life balance, but the month you join is one of the most critical times to be visibly in the office and working long (critical project crunch time and the month of performance assessments being the other two key times).

2. Figure out how to optimize your development environment. The raw language you work most with may not change (Java, for example) but the development environment may be very different from what you are used to. The way you check out, review, deploy, test, and even the IDE you use may change with a new job. Try to identify the most proficient engineers (frequency and size of code reviews--easy metrics) and ask what tools they use to make them more efficient. But if you can see a way to bring tricks or tools from your previous work in, don't be shy. I saw a dramatic shift from Eclipse to IntelliJ in one of my teams after a couple of new engineers came in from other companies and demonstrated to the old-timers some of the advantages they were seeing.

3. Quiet competence wins. You were hired for this company because they think you have something to offer, but let your actions speak louder than your words. When you come in and either ask a ton of questions without thought or start dispensing advice in the wrong context, you are going to put some distance between yourself and your new team. Far better to spend the first couple of months getting the lay of the land and producing awesome work than trying to rock a boat you know nothing about or badgering people with questions you can find answers to on your own.

4. Understand what matters to your manager. The most important relationship you will have at work will be with your manager. You want him or her to trust you and to recognize the work that you are doing. Find out what matters to them either by directly asking them in one of your first couple of 1:1s or by observing their behavior in meetings and interactions. What is your manager measuring, either explicitly or implicitly? Do they notice extra hours? Clever code? Innovative ideas? Number of support tickets resolved? Thorough code reviews? Clear status reports? Find what it is that matters to your manager and be sure you are optimizing to it. This sounds like pandering and it probably is, but your job is going to be much happier if you understand what matters most. That doesn't mean that is all you optimize for and it doesn't mean you don't have the freedom so loved by engineers, but knowing the rules of the game makes it much easier to win - or at least not lose.

5. Make the most of 1:1s. Your manager should be setting up weekly or biweekly 1:1s with you to discuss your performance, projects, and whatever else is on your minds. Make sure to go into these 1:1s with an agenda. Sometimes that agenda will be feedback you want on a design, sometimes it will be an idea to

improve things, sometimes it will just be highlighting to your manager something interesting you have been working on. Engineers who and just silently shrug their way through these meetings are wasting valuable time for both parties.

6. Record your work. Nothing is going to make performance reviews easier for you (and by extension, for your manager) than keeping a weekly record of your achievements. Every Friday, before you leave for the weekend, record somewhere (OneNote works really well for this but vi or emacs is perfectly fine as well) not just what you did (completed piece X or project Y) but also some of the relevant metrics. Did you introduce a new feature? Record relevant counters like the performance improvements, customer impact, customer feedback quotes, etc. Did you resolve the root cause of a customer issue? Record some of the customer complaints or internal issues that were caused by it. Also record links to design documents, code reviews, meeting notes, etc. This all feels like overhead, but these 5-10 minutes are going to be extremely valuable as you write your performance review at the end of the year and will give your manager the data they need to justify giving you a great rating. It also will help give you perspective as you go from week 1 to week 101 to appreciate the scope and impact of your work.

7. Make friends. It sounds kind of sick but for five days of the week, you are probably going to see more of your teammates than you will your spouse, your kids, your dog, or anyone else. You are going to be seeing lots of them, and if you like each other, you are going to love life a lot more. Spend the time to get to know them over lunch and in casual conversation, and genuinely be interested in them. Maybe it's something as simple as bringing snacks to the candy or snacks to work. Simple things like that sound small but will help you gain

rapport with your team members. The gestures won't go unnoticed.

The first couple of months are going to be overwhelming with a new environment, potentially moving to a new city, and pressure to perform. Put in the extra time and effort, though, and you'll establish the right kind of reputation--the kind that takes less effort to maintain than it does to establish.

Beyond the Beginning

Once you have made it through the first 90 days and made the right impression, you can take your foot off the accelerator a bit and try to establish a routine that will be sustainable over the many years to come. For a small number of developers, just coasting is good enough, and as long as you keep performing, that may fine with your company. If you are interested in advancing, though, there are some activities you should pay attention to that will make that path smooth.

Find a Mentor
It is important that you establish not just informal mentors and a network of experts you can rely on, but also a mentor who is outside your immediate team that you can meet with regularly. Mentors are important for a couple of reasons. First, they can provide another perspective on the company and your place within the company. Second, they can give you personal advice on your weaknesses and strengths and work with you on a path to improvement. Third, a mentor ideally should be someone with specific skills you want to learn from, since they can help you improve in that area. Lastly, mentors are often a great source of recruiting; many internal transfers happen along mentoring lines.

I have had a series of mentors throughout the places I've worked. Setting up a mentorship does not need to be a huge deal - this isn't a lifelong marriage contract. Early on in my career, for example, I knew I needed to beef up on my unit testing practices and tools so I reached out to another software developer in the company who was very active on quality/testing mailings lists. For a year or so I met with him monthly, worked with him on real projects I was developing, and learned a great deal. After a year, though, I had learned most of the skills he had excelled at and we both agreed it was time to move on.

Even after your regular meetings are finished, though, a mentor will remain a valuable long-term part of your network.

Specialize in Something

As a manager, the most valuable software developers I had were those who were competent and willing to take on any task, but also were experts on specific areas. Jacks-of-all-trades rarely get promoted to senior level positions. You need to be known for something. To be clear, I'm not suggesting switching away from the general software developer role, but within that role find something that interests you and at which you can be the best on your team. Some ideas include:

- Data expertise - Knowing how to store and query data, particularly at large scale, is valuable on just about every team. Be the person your team turns to when they need to run a query or design a database.

- Testing - There is a wealth of testing tools and practices and plenty of room to get great at this area. Don't just write great unit tests on your own, though. Make it easier for others to as well, and make testing an easy and powerful part of your team process.

- Machine Learning - Working with Big Data is an increasingly common need at tech companies and this in an area that a lot of new graduates seem to have a passion for. Many companies have specific machine learning roles like Data Scientist, Machine Learning Engineer, and Research Scientist, but being a software developer who also happens to know how to pull answers out of the noise of data is going to get you noticed.

- Web Development - Building a performant data store and complex business logic is great, but if it doesn't look good on a user's web browser or doesn't perform quickly when rendered, all that backend work is wasted. Software developers with a web focus will not only understand how to write the full software stack, but will know HTML, CSS, and JavaScript and put that to expert use in creating beautiful, fast, and responsive websites. For whatever reason, this is a skillset that is surprisingly uncommon in the teams I've worked on. The engineers who have this expertise are in very high demand.

- Project Management - For developers who enjoy some managing of projects without all of the overhead of a full Technical Program Manager or Software Development Manager role, having a knack for organization can be valuable. When a manager or project manager is overloaded, they need a developer with an inside knowledge of the project and team who can help prioritize and assign tasks, clear roadblocks, and keep things on track.

- Security - Developers who are passionate about security are usually a little odd (even for engineers), but someone who really understands attack vectors and prevention is also respected. Don't just be the security guy who tells everyone how broken their software is. Also be the one to provide the mitigation and you'll be valued in your team and company.

- Quality and Detail Authority - This one is a little less defined, but acute attention to detail and very high standards are skills that are valued and recognized. Be the one that everyone trusts to review the most critical parts of projects and you'll have an important spot in your team and your manager's mind.

There are many other areas to specialize in but you've got to pick at least one to make it very far. Don't neglect your core role as a software developer, but find something beyond that to keep you learning and make a name for yourself.

Take on Extra-Curriculars

While it is true that there are some developers who are going to be happy to just let their career happen, if you want to increase your exposure, recognition, and chances of promotion, you are going to have to go beyond your core responsibilities. As discussed above, the first step is going to be finding areas to specialize in. To take that a step further, however, you should look for causes to be involved in that go beyond your core team. Often times there are pre-existing organizations like this within a company, but if not, there is no reason not to start your own. Being involved in these organizations will broaden your network, increase your reputation, and help you stand out against others. Some of the extra-curricular areas I've seen that you could consider are:

- Hiring and Interviewing - Beyond just doing normal interviews, which is an expectation of most software developers, many companies have specialized roles for the best interviewers to help keep the quality of new hires high. At Google, there is a hiring committee of managers and senior engineers. At Amazon, there are Bar Raisers who have veto power on any interview loop. Even at companies without formal interviewer recognition, having the reputation as a fantastic interviewer will help you stand out.

- Book Clubs - Many people want to further their engineering skills but will be more motivated if they do it with a group. Organize a book club by soliciting for interested engineers and then picking a book or chapter or online course to study for a month and then review and discuss. Chances are, if you can sell it right then not only will it be beneficial for you and the other engineers, but your company will be willing to pitch in to pay for the study materials. The time commitment for you is low and this is an easy way to stand out as a facilitator of engineering improvement.

- Brownbags and Conferences - If you can handle public speaking, look for opportunities to share your knowledge with others in brownbag discussions. Often times there are brownbags organized by different groups (testing groups, front-end engineering groups, database groups, security groups, business/tech groups) and they are always looking for speakers. Many companies will also have all-day or half-day internal conferences around topics. Look for ways to be involved in the organization of these events, or give a presentation there.

- Design Review Committees - Amazon has a tradition of organizing "samurai" groups that are made up of mid and senior engineers in an organization who give presentations and who act as a design review committee. Being involved with groups like these gives you exposure to what else is happening in the organization as well as interaction with top talent who can be useful for mentoring and feedback.

- Affinity Groups - Affinity groups are a great way for employees to help people that may be under-represented by the mainstream organization. If you belong to one of these affinity groups or simply want to help reach out and support individuals affiliated from a group, look to join or start one of these programs in your company. While just being a member of one of these groups probably isn't going to directly help your career, taking a leadership role in one of these programs is a way to gain organizational skills, support other employees, and aid in recruiting efforts.

- Patents - This can be a touchy subject for some engineers, as there are a number of companies that seem to abuse the patent system by using patents as a way not just to protect intellectual investment but to cast a wide net on ideas and try to milk any companies who are doing well. If you trust your company to not be one of those, it would be advantageous to you and your career to think about whether or not what you are doing could be patented. Any large tech company will have an intellectual property department that will work with you to turn your idea into a patent application. Although the company will own the patent, it will be another point to stand out in your company and something that will continue with you on your resume.

- Publications - If your company allows it (which isn't always the case) and you have the time either through work or on the side, publishing a work in the tech space is another way to stand out. Make sure your company is on board, though, and re-read through your contracts.

- External Events - If you have become expert enough in your field, look for opportunities to represent your work and your company at conferences and other external events. It is fairly uncommon for engineers to be comfortable enough to present in front of a large group, but if you are, this is a great way to get your name known beyond just your company.

Before you start investing a lot of time in one of these additional pursuits, make sure your manager is also on board. You usually don't strictly need their permission and there would have to be extraordinary circumstances for them not to be enthusiastically on board, but you should do them the courtesy of letting them know of additional demands on your time.

Sustainable Working

Software development should be a career that can be very sustainable and there is a lot of room to find happiness in the kinds of work you do. While most of the career advice in this book has been focused on gaining skills and recognition, understand that this is a marathon, not a sprint, and recognition is not going to be worth more than loving the job you have. By managing your time, interests, and finances, you'll be able to have an enjoyable long-term career in software development.

Working in software development is a lot like having a new baby. When the baby sleeps, you should sleep; when the baby is screaming, you are going to need to get up too. There will be times throughout the year when a project or your own development needs a bit extra from you. A week or two of late nights, a few weekends, all of this is pretty normal and commensurate with the pay you are receiving. To make that sustainable, though, you need to also rest "when the baby rests." Take advantage of the flexibility that most tech workplaces allow and skip out a bit early some days to take care of appointments or surprise your family by an early arrival home. If you are getting your work done and are present when the team is all-on-deck, no good manager is going to quibble about the hours you work in a day. If they do, or if you are in a team or company that demands you are always there all the time, then get out. Life is too short and there is too much demand for engineers for you to feel trapped at a job that doesn't appreciate you.

Most software development, by nature, is creative and doesn't get boring as quickly as many other jobs. Still, if you find the work you are doing uninteresting, it may be time to look around. I would suggest you first look at yourself to see what has changed. Have you mastered the domain space you are working on? Have you become the most senior person and are missing some role models? Has your business stopped innovating and the work become mostly operational? Figure out what you are missing and first see if it is something you can fix within yourself. If you need to look beyond, looking around at other teams within your company is the lowest-friction way to make a change and is usually supported as long as you've been in your current team for a year or two (I recommend at least two to three years in a team). Use the network you have established and mentors you have found and try to find an area that interests you and that is run by someone you like and respect. If there are fundamental problems you have with your company (type of work, compensation, work demands, etc.), then certainly look elsewhere - it might be time to pay attention again to all those LinkedIn nags that recruiters are sending you. Whether you transfer internally or externally, be sure that you have a secure offer in-hand before you talk with your manager. Once you have announced your intent to leave, your manager may personally still like you and want the best for you, but their responsibility is to start looking past you to who will fill your spot.

With the high pay common in most software development jobs and the practical tastes that many engineers have, software development is a great career for those seeking to retire a bit earlier than normal, to enjoy long sabbaticals, or to otherwise have less money-stress in life. How you spend your money is of course a personal choice, but I'd advise you to apply a small amount of the rigor and planning that you put into your career into planning your personal finances. As awesome as software development is, you may someday want to pursue a new pursuit (or develop software without the need for pay), and a nest egg will allow you that freedom.

For the foreseeable future, software development looks to remain a well-paid, high-demand, and highly satisfying career. If you have the aptitude, hard work, and a bit of luck, you can enjoy the fruits of a fantastic job that can help provide a fantastic life.

Enjoy the journey!

Further Reading

Interview Preparation
McDowell, Gayle Laakmann. Cracking the coding interview: 150 programming interview questions and solutions. CareerCup. http://amzn.to/1sErxoy

Aziz, Adnan, and Amit Prakash. Elements of Programming Interviews: The Insiders' Guide. http://amzn.to/1weA4QH

Skiena, Steven S.. The Algorithm Design Manual. TELOS--the Electronic Library of Science. http://amzn.to/1t14s0M

The Software Engineering Craft
Bloch, Joshua. Effective Java. Addison-Wesley. http://amzn.to/1psqR24

Freeman, Eric, Elisabeth Freeman, Kathy Sierra, and Bert Bates. Head First Design Patterns. O'Reilly. http://amzn.to/1okQiHX

Hunt, Andrew, and David Thomas. The Pragmatic Programmer: From Journeyman to Master. Addison-Wesley. http://amzn.to/1Foh47m

McConnell, Steve. Code Complete: A Practical Handbook of Software Construction. Microsoft Press. http://amzn.to/1wiFtW6

Martin, Robert. Clean Code: A Handbook of Agile Software Craftsmanship. Prentice Hall. http://amzn.to/1Gi45op

Career Advice
Fowler, Chad, and Chad Fowler. The Passionate Programmer: Creating a Remarkable Career in Software Development. Pragmatic Bookshelf. http://amzn.to/1psquov

www.ingramcontent.com/pod-product-compliance
Lightning Source LLC
Chambersburg PA
CBHW061032050326
40689CB00012B/2776